We Are All Different

We All Read

Rebecca Rissman

www.heinemannlibrary.co.uk
Visit our website to find out more information about Heinemann Library books.

To order:
 Phone 44 (0) 1865 888066
 Send a fax to 44 (0) 1865 314091
 Visit the Heinemann Bookshop at www.heinemannlibrary.co.uk to browse our catalogue and order online.

Heinemann Library is an imprint of Capstone Global Library Limited, a company incorporated in England and Wales having its registered office at 7 Pilgrim Street, London, EC4V 6LB – Registered company number: 6695582

Heinemann is a registered trademark of Pearson Education Limited, under licence to Capstone Global Library Limited

Text © Capstone Global Library Limited 2009
First published in hardback in 2009
The moral rights of the proprietor have been asserted.

Edited by Rebecca Rissman, Charlotte Guillain and Catherine Veitch
Designed by Joanna Hinton-Malivoire
Picture research by Tracy Cummins
Production by Duncan Gilbert
Originated by Dot Gradations Ltd
Printed and bound in China by South China Printing Company Ltd

ISBN 978 0 431 19312 0 (hardback)
13 12 11 10 09
10 9 8 7 6 5 4 3 2 1

British Library Cataloguing in Publication Data
Rissman, Rebecca
We all read. - (We are all different)
1. People with disabilities - Juvenile literature
2. Literacy - Juvenile literature
305.9'08
A full catalogue record for this book is available from the British Library.

Acknowledgements
We would like to thank the following for permission to reproduce photographs: ©agefotostock pp. **19** (John Birdsall), **22** (Banana Stock); ©Alamy p. **20** (David Lyons); ©Corbis pp. **9** (Paul Barton), **12** (zefa/Brigitte Sporrer); ©drr.net pp. **10** (Brett Snow), **18** (Anderson Ross), **21** (Design Pics/ Kristy-Anne Glubish); ©Getty Images pp. **4** (Tay Rees), **6** (Jose Luis Pelaez Inc.), **7** (Image Source), **8** (Abid Katib), **15** (China Photos), **16** (AFP PHOTO/LIU Jin), **23 middle** (Abid Katib), **23 bottom** (China Photos); ©Ladov pp. **14** (REUTERS/Crack Palinggi), **23 top** (Reuters/Crack Palinggi); ©shutterstock pp. **11** (Jose AS Reyes), **13** (Nir Levy), **17** (Matka Wariatka).

Cover photograph of a blind boy reading Braille, in Shenyang reproduced with permission of ©Landov (Xinhua). Back cover photograph of a college student in a wheelchair reproduced with permission of ©drr.net (Anderson Ross).

Every effort has been made to contact copyright holders of material reproduced in this book. Any omissions will be rectified in subsequent printings if notice is given to the publishers.

Contents

Differences

We are all different ages and sizes. We all have different coloured hair and skin. We are all good at different things.

Reading

We read words.

We read sentences.

Sometimes we read to learn. Some
people need glasses to read.

Sometimes we read for fun.
Sometimes people read to us.

How we read

People read in different ways.

People read in different places.

Some people read from left to right.

Some people read from right to left.

Braille

Some people read with their fingers.

headphones

Some people listen to sounds to help them read words on a screen.

character

Some people read characters.

Some people read letters.

What we read

Sometimes people read books.

Sometimes people read newspapers.

Sometimes people read signs.

Sometimes people read
using computers.

We are all different

There are lots of different ways to read. How do you read?

Words to know

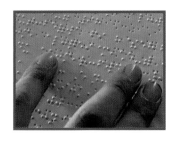 **Braille** raised bumps on paper. People read Braille with their fingers.

 **glasses** small pieces of glass worn over the eyes. Glasses help some people see.

 **headphones** small speakers people wear over or inside the ears. Headphones help people hear.

Index

Note to parents and teachers

Before reading

Talk about the ways people are the same and different. Some of the differences are physical or mental, and some are because different people like different things – but all people are special and all people are equally important. Ask the children why they think it is important to learn to read. Point out that we don't only read books: we can read from a whiteboard, a computer, magazines, and words on signs and on television.

After reading

Show the children some examples of Braille, and let them feel the raised dots. Help them make their own "Braille" letters by piercing holes in the shape of letters through thin card. Turn the cards over and see if they can "read" the letters.